SeaKids Workbook

Lee Ann Mancini and Kirsten Rangel

SeaKidsTV.com

Sea Kids Workbook
For Books and Animation Episodes 1 -26

GLM Publishing LLC
P.O. Box 812633
Boca Raton, Florida 33431

SeaKidsTV.com
© 2019 GLM Publishing LLC
© Characters ownership and licensing by
P23 Entertainment Inc.

ISBN# 978-0-9973325-4-4

Manufactured in the USA

Library of Congress Control Number
2019910454

"Train up a child in the way he should go,
Even when he is old he will not depart from it"
Proverbs 22:6 (NASB).

Table of Contents

Introduction

Dear Parent/Teacher/Ministry Leader,

We hope you will find this educational resource guide to be an effective tool to help solidify the biblical principles being taught in the books and in the animation series.

Some suggestions while using this workbook:

• All of our books are on the free app, Novel Effect, which enhances the stories by using music and sound effects to bring them to life. Children love to hear the sounds and music each story brings while they read.

• For the animation series: Read the quizzes before viewing each episode. This way, the children know what to look for and what to pay attention to.

• For the discussion questions: Most are open-ended and allow responses that include information about feelings, ideas, and attitudes, in addition to comprehension of biblical principles.

• For the word searches: Be sure to discuss the words and their meanings on each sheet. For older children, have them write out a sentence or look up a Bible verse for each word, indicating that they understand the meaning and usage of the word. All verses referenced are from the NASB.

All episodes are available on Right Now Media, Pure Flix, and Trinity Broadcasting Network. Individual DVDs are available for purchase at SeaKidsTV.com.

Please pray for our mission to create products and resources that help revolutionize how we indoctrinate biblical principles and the love of Jesus into children; educating them in a tangible way so they can learn through their experiences as they practice what is being taught.

In His Service and for His Glory,

Lee Ann Mancini & Kirsten Rangel

A Servant Like Jesus
Quiz

1. What problem did Charlie face on his first day of school?
   a. He was shy
   b. He argued with a classmate
   c. Sea Kids made fun of him
   d. He bragged about his toys

2. Where did Charlie hide?
   a. Behind the toy bin
   b. Under the table
   c. In the bathroom
   d. Behind the cleanup sink

3. Who did Charlie save on his class field trip?
   a. Miss Stella
   b. Bernie
   c. Tina
   d. Willie

4. What did Charlie pray for on his class field trip?
   a. A new lunchbox
   b. More friends
   c. For courage to save his friend
   d. To go home

Bible verses for discussion:
   1 Timothy 4:12
   *Proverbs 5:21
   Philippians 2:4
   1 Corinthians 16:13
*Memory verse

A Servant Like Jesus
Discussion Questions

1. Why do you think some Sea Kids cried on their first day of school?

2. Why did Willy and Tina have an argument?

3. What did Charlie whisper in Miss Stella's ear? Why do you think he whispered?

4. Do you think Charlie was scared, shy, or both, on his first day of school?

5. What did Charlie do when Miss Stella asked him to be her helper?

6. What happened to Bernie on the field trip? What did Charlie do?

7. At the field trip, what was Charlie's prayer to Jesus?

8. What did Charlie do in the classroom and at home to show that he can also be a servant like Jesus?

9. How can you be a servant like Jesus?

10. What prayer do you say every night to Jesus?

A Servant Like Jesus
Word Search

```
H  E  L  P  E  R  M  G  K  P  C  E  E  Z  V
Y  A  P  K  E  L  C  O  B  A  C  N  Y  J  L
S  E  C  A  Q  A  S  O  O  E  I  R  H  U  J
O  G  R  H  L  X  Q  E  U  J  R  S  H  Y  S
A  Q  Z  S  A  O  F  Q  F  R  E  N  J  F  Y
K  Y  G  E  U  R  Z  F  N  Q  A  S  I  Y  K
Q  K  Y  R  I  T  L  Z  R  Y  T  G  U  E  Q
T  P  S  V  W  E  I  F  I  I  Z  E  S  H
A  X  Q  A  F  A  O  B  E  N  E  J  L  X  R
S  R  A  N  K  C  P  R  U  C  Z  N  S  B  G
Z  T  R  T  O  H  R  Q  Z  H  L  U  D  M  K
O  R  I  N  U  E  A  S  F  E  D  A  P  S  T
Y  O  K  N  R  R  Y  F  Z  J  L  B  S  B  Z
N  H  N  M  G  O  E  H  R  H  P  Q  M  S  G
I  B  X  V  R  X  R  U  I  E  Z  B  H  Z  X
```

Helper	Servant	Teacher
Jesus	Friends	Prayer
Bernie	Courage	Class
Sting	Charlie	Shy

Fast Freddy
Quiz

1. How did Freddy feel on his first day of school?
   a. Happy
   b. Sad
   c. Excited
   d. Angry

2. Who explained that making fun of someone just because they are different is not nice?
   a. Joey
   b. Freddy
   c. Danny
   d. Miss Linda Mermaid

3. Who helped the Catfish Cruisers win the championship?
   a. Coach Crab
   b. Freddy
   c. Danny
   d. Marcus

4. What did Freddy pray for at the end of the story?
   a. For another pizza
   b. To be better than everyone else on the team
   c. For another trophy
   d. For being different and special, and for all his new friends

Bible verses for discussion:
*1 Peter 5:7
Colossians 3:12
Philippians 4:19
Galatians 6:9
*Memory verse

Fast Freddy
Discussion Questions

1. How do you think Freddy felt on his first day of school?

2. Why were the Sea Kids staring at Freddy?

3. Why did the Sea Kids think Freddy "looked weird?"

4. What could have the Sea Kids done to make Freddy feel better?

5. What do you think gave Freddy the courage to speak up and tell the class that

   he was a great swimmer and wrestler?

6. Why did the Sea Kids start to like Freddy?

7. Do you know anyone like Marcus? How can you help him/her to be nicer?

8. Was Freddy happier he won the race or happier he had new friends?

9. What do you pray to Jesus about every night?

10. How can you help someone fit in and not feel left out? What would Jesus do?

Fast Freddy
Word Search

I	M	I	V	H	S	S	R	P	S	Y	N	M	G	O
B	N	X	D	E	B	P	V	I	E	M	A	A	F	Y
B	M	E	R	M	A	I	D	Z	S	M	T	R	B	J
P	G	H	C	O	A	C	H	Z	T	C	G	C	A	Q
R	P	V	P	E	N	B	G	A	C	D	W	U	K	B
A	W	J	E	S	U	S	L	N	J	F	E	S	F	R
Y	I	G	Q	C	J	W	I	N	N	E	R	C	A	O
A	F	K	D	E	T	Y	P	Y	S	W	T	B	S	F
Z	G	V	S	F	R	N	B	G	K	I	L	I	T	L
E	I	C	A	M	O	Q	F	Q	E	V	N	M	S	W
T	E	A	M	M	P	Q	R	G	Z	Z	J	T	I	T
X	C	O	U	N	H	G	E	U	Q	K	I	S	S	M
R	S	S	L	J	Y	W	D	C	J	G	U	M	U	W
C	A	T	P	F	G	P	D	D	A	N	N	Y	S	Q
X	H	T	S	T	O	V	Y	M	V	N	Q	C	E	B

Danny	Mermaid	Trophy
Jesus	Winner	Coach
Pray	Freddy	Fast
Pizza	Marcus	Team

I'm Not Afraid!
Quiz

1. What ride was Susie afraid of?
   a. Lobster Circle Basket
   b. Starfish Ferris Wheel
   c. Whale-Back Roller Coaster
   d. The water slides

2. How did Susie first act when Rachel asked to ride the roller coaster?
   a. She made Rachel eat food and play games
   b. She left the park
   c. She called her friend
   d. She went on the Roller Coaster

3. What did Susie do after speaking to her mom?
   a. She told Rachel she wanted to leave
   b. She played more games
   c. She prayed to Jesus and went on the ride
   d. She ate more food

4. What lesson did Susie learn?
   a. It is not okay to be afraid
   b. Jesus turns your fear into faith
   c. To always make excuses
   d. All of the above

Bible verses for discussion:
   Isaiah 43:5
   Philippians 4:6
   Mark 5:36
   *Psalm 34:4
*Memory verse

I'm Not Afraid!
Discussion Questions

1. Why do you think Susie was making excuses not to go on the roller coaster?

2. Why did Susie call her mother? What did her mother tell her to do?

3. What did Susie do just before the ride took off?

4. How did Jesus answer her prayer?

5. Why did Susie want to ride the roller coaster again and again?

6. According to Rachel, who is the best friend anyone can have?

7. Is Jesus your best friend? How do you know?

8. What are you afraid of?

9. How can you help a friend overcome their fears?

10. What things can you do the next time you are afraid?

Name:_____   Date:_____

I'm Not Afraid!
Word Search

B	D	B	A	M	H	V	Y	I	J	E	S	U	S	P
B	I	Z	H	Q	C	K	S	F	O	S	H	B	O	E
F	I	P	T	A	J	C	U	W	D	W	Y	A	T	H
M	B	V	O	Y	D	O	S	F	F	A	I	T	H	D
K	V	J	Y	R	F	U	I	X	A	L	B	T	W	S
A	M	P	S	F	W	R	E	G	I	F	W	P	G	R
L	Z	Z	F	C	T	A	Q	F	X	W	R	R	R	M
Y	C	M	O	Y	Y	G	T	K	T	M	L	A	U	C
S	G	V	O	N	C	E	H	E	P	A	G	Y	I	H
J	Z	X	D	J	O	Q	R	S	R	N	X	E	P	D
X	S	X	M	B	G	P	E	O	R	P	Z	R	F	J
Q	B	E	F	R	I	E	N	D	S	B	A	W	I	C
U	R	A	C	H	E	L	B	O	M	U	H	R	I	T
N	W	T	C	R	I	D	E	S	E	S	S	K	K	O
W	I	X	Z	C	M	M	W	G	Y	T	O	R	N	O

Water Park   Rides   Afraid

Courage   Faith   Rachel

Friends   Susie   Toys

Prayer   Jesus   Food

15

Forever With Jesus
Quiz

1. What did Jesus die for?
   a. For the animals
   b. For His sins
   c. For our sins
   d. All of the above

2. What were the children building outside?
   a. Sandcastles
   b. Blocks
   c. 3-D puzzles
   d. Tents

3. What are the streets of heaven lined with?
   a. Seashells
   b. Gold
   c. Pearls
   d. Coral

4. Who reads to the children to teach them about heaven?
   a. Grandpa
   b. Mrs. Higgins
   c. Grandma Pinky
   d. Pastor Gage

Bible verses discussion:
*Romans 3:23
John 14:2-3
Revelation 21:21
Psalm 92:14
*Memory verse

Forever With Jesus
Discussion Questions

1. Why do you think the Sea Kids were sad about Mr. Higgins' death?

2. What do you think heaven will be like?

3. Why do you think some children are afraid of death?

4. What did Jesus do in order for us to live with Him in heaven forever?

5. What do the words "sin" and "salvation" mean?

6. What can you do to make someone feel better when they are sad?

7. Explain what this sentence means: "When you believe in Jesus, you never die."

8. How can we forgive others who have sinned against us?

9. How is family important to you?

10. Explain what the word "forever" means.

Forever With Jesus
Word Search

```
W  T  W  T  C  Z  T  R  G  X  G  V  X  W  O
W  X  C  F  F  C  M  D  J  Y  U  H  C  W  G
D  F  I  U  T  M  F  I  E  G  A  E  N  V  R
P  C  O  J  M  H  Y  O  S  C  G  H  C  K  A
E  A  V  R  H  K  J  C  U  F  F  L  X  V  N
A  P  S  D  E  S  K  S  S  C  K  L  N  A  D
V  U  R  T  Z  V  C  O  I  O  J  P  E  W  P
K  A  O  A  O  D  E  K  F  U  K  E  W  D  A
K  G  G  S  Y  R  W  R  A  S  F  S  V  L  N
X  K  S  O  I  Y  S  P  M  I  E  R  H  U  F
J  D  I  X  L  M  R  P  I  N  T  K  T  T  A
J  O  N  I  O  D  Z  W  L  S  J  K  K  T  R
T  D  M  O  P  X  H  T  Y  V  M  E  T  H  H
F  P  I  N  K  Y  A  L  C  A  S  T  L  E  H
U  W  Y  V  H  E  A  V  E  N  F  D  E  S  M
```

Forever	Family	Castle
Grandpa	Pastor	Jesus
Cousins	Pinky	Pray
Heaven	Sin	Gold

18

Name:_____   Date:_____

What a Bragger!
Quiz

1. What was Melissa bragging about?
   a. Having more toys than anyone
   b. Swimming the fastest
   c. Talking the loudest
   d. All of the above

2. What idea did Corey have for Melissa's birthday?
   a. Buying her a gift with the help of other Sea Kids
   b. Baking a cake for Melissa
   c. Taking her to the toy store
   d. Introducing her to Snappy Cat Starfish

3. Why did Melissa cry when she opened her present?
   a. Because she was sad
   b. Because she was angry
   c. Because she was scared
   d. Because she was happy

4. What was Melissa's prayer before she went to bed?
   a. Thanking Jesus for her stuffed toy
   b. Thanking Jesus for her glasses
   c. Thanking Jesus for her mommy, daddy, family, and friends
   d. Thanking Jesus for her presents

Bible verses for discussion:
*1 Corinthians 1:31
Matthew 10:42
Psalm 126:5
Psalm 106:1
*Memory verse

What a Bragger!
Discussion Questions

1. What is bragging?

2. What did Melissa brag about? Why do you think she bragged?

3. How did it make you feel when Melissa was crying in the sandbox?

   Why was she crying?

4. Why did Corey thank Jesus for all his toys?

5. What nice thing did Mr. Wilbur do?

6. How do you think Melissa felt when she knew her friends had a

   present for her? Why did she cry?

7. How did Melissa show her appreciation for what her friends did?

8. Have you ever bragged about something?

9. How can you help a friend not to brag?

10. Why is bragging a sin?

Name:_____   Date:_____

What a Bragger!
Word Search

```
Y M Y T X L O V P R F C S U B
B C K W C F D V Z N K W S E Y
R A T V Q M E L I S S A M I U
A K H P R E S E N T P S A J I
G E A V B X W J U I R B V R L
F H N C I I S W E N A V R P K
B D K I S G R Z N S Y J S U V
L C F M G Q Y T U I U Z Y T P
V O U F S I G V H D M S Y K K
G R L R L E T G M D U A W I V
Q E J I E Y S O W K A P G E V
L Y R E Y W K T Y O N Y J J E
Y O W N U I A Z J S M V V M W
B G K D K E V Z P U T P A Q L
Q N T S N Q G S H O V E L J O
```

Jesus	Birthday	Present
Corey	Thankful	Shovel
Cake	Melissa	Toys
Brag	Friends	Pray

God's Gift
Quiz

1. What did Christian and Jacob argue about?
   a. Who had more friends
   b. Who could swim faster
   c. Who got more toys at Christmas/Hanukkah
   d. Who was taller

2. What is the most important gift from God at Christmas?
   a. Gift of light
   b. Presents
   c. Santa Claus
   d. Gift of our Messiah, Jesus

3. What is the most important gift from God at Hanukkah?
   a. Presents
   b. Star of David
   c. Gift of light
   d. Jesus

4. What do Christian and Jacob pray for in the end?
   a. More toys
   b. A new bike
   c. Mommy, Daddy, their families, and friends
   d. A new lunch box

Bible verses for discussion:
   *Philippians 2:14
   Luke 2:11
   Psalm 23:1
   1 John 5:14
*Memory verse

Name:_____ Date:_____

God's Gift
Discussion Questions

1. What did the Sea Kids help their parents do outside their homes?

2. What did Christian place in the manger? Why did he have to be careful?

3. Why did some caves have Christmas trees and some have menorahs?

4. Why were Jacob and Christian arguing on the playground?

5. What were Christian's and Jacob's prayers at the end?

6. What is a manger? What is a menorah?

7. What do you think Christmas and Hanukkah are about?

8. What are you thankful for?

9. Why should we always love others as God loves us?

10. What other holidays do you celebrate?

God's Gift
Word Search

```
V Q E Z M H L U A Z O R Q U J
E X Z I R O Y U J Z N P N Z F
Y I E V F A M I L Y K E L Q K
J E S U S O L F Y A M A K A M
X M W L B Q M R P P J K F T A
R F X T C Q E I J E H S I U N
C R B T L W N E O D K B T Q G
H H K P C F O N L H E P B O E
R D X B V R R D I A E B H N R
I U L Y G G A S G N S T O S J
S W P J M O H H H U P G L P J
T D M W C D S I T K K I I F I
M K V Q P K R P S K O V D Z V
A N V M I S T A R A J V A T X
S T P U A E B V B H U N Y Z H
```

Manger   Friendship   Holiday

Jesus   Christmas   Family

Yamaka   Hanukkah   Star

Lights   Menorah   God

24

Name:_____   Date:_____

God's Easter Miracles
Quiz

1. Who witnessed an Easter miracle?
   a. Jimmy
   b. Paul
   c. Lenny
   d. All of the above

2. What did Paul learn?
   a. Finding Easter eggs is important
   b. Giving is better than receiving
   c. Easter is about getting candy
   d. Easter is about getting presents

3. Why did the class pray for Lenny?
   a. He was sick
   b. He lost his toy
   c. He was hit by a boat propeller
   d. He was bullied

4. What is Easter about?
   a. Easter Bunny
   b. Easter eggs
   c. Easter egg hunt
   d. Jesus giving up His life for our sins

Bible verses for discussion:
   Jeremiah 32:27
   Acts 20:35
   Jeremiah 17:14
   *Romans 10:9-10
*Memory verse

God's Easter Miracles
Discussion Questions

1. What Easter game did the Sea Kids play in the story?

2. How did Paul act when he didn't find one of the special Easter eggs?

3. Why did Jimmy think it was not fair to share one of his special eggs?

4. Why did the class have to pray for Brian's little brother, Lenny?

5. What did Jimmy ask his father? What was his father's answer?

6. What special prayer did Jimmy say?

7. What Easter miracles did God give Jimmy and Lenny?

8. What did Paul give Lenny in the hospital? Why did he give it to Lenny?

9. Why is Easter special?

10. How do you celebrate Easter?

Name:_____   Date:_____

God's Easter Miracles
Word Search

```
Y  L  B  P  F  T  X  G  H  P  M  M  N  D  X
V  L  E  N  N  Y  C  S  E  O  D  I  C  O  A
V  S  K  X  J  Y  W  U  A  A  M  R  J  Q  C
W  Y  T  P  H  J  N  N  V  P  Q  A  G  N  O
Q  F  H  A  R  R  R  D  E  E  N  C  G  Z  O
T  Y  T  J  P  A  B  A  N  E  E  L  O  R  I
G  J  Z  I  R  I  Y  Y  C  G  A  E  R  J  C
L  G  J  M  E  T  B  E  A  G  S  S  D  O  M
H  O  E  M  P  Y  B  A  R  H  T  N  G  B  P
Y  D  S  Y  Z  J  E  S  J  U  E  V  S  J  Y
L  A  U  T  I  S  M  V  U  N  R  Q  F  X  F
Q  I  S  H  X  P  I  Y  D  T  Y  Z  Z  E  Y
T  W  M  N  W  A  W  L  M  H  V  W  X  F  N
A  Y  E  U  O  U  J  R  S  Y  P  B  J  D  K
V  H  S  B  X  L  V  N  P  Z  M  T  V  B  L
```

Autism	Miracles	Sunday
Jesus	Egg Hunt	Prayer
Jimmy	Easter	Paul
Lenny	Heaven	God

Respect Effect
Matching Quiz

A.    B.   C.    D.

Match the character to his/her description. Choose one Bible verse from the box that best applies to each statement.

_____ 1. This character teaches her class about honoring

your mother and father. Bible verse:

_____ 2. This character becomes a bad influence on David.

Bible verse:

_____ 3. This character says, "When you disrespect your parents,

it is a sin against God." Bible verse:

_____ 4. This character learns the importance of obeying his

parents. Bible verse:

Bible verses to choose from:
Romans 13:2
Proverbs 1:5
*Ephesians 6:1-3
1 Corinthians 15:33
*Memory verse

Respect Effect
Discussion Questions

1. Why was David not paying attention in class?

2. Why do you think Marcus said, "You church kids aren't exactly my type?"

3. Why did Christian not want to learn anything from Marcus?

4. What prank did David pull on Christian? How did it make Christian feel?

5. How did Marcus take advantage of his friendship with David?

6. What did David do that caused his mother to punish him?

7. Why did Christian pray to Jesus for his friend, David?

8. When David prayed to Jesus, how did Jesus help David?

9. What does it mean to honor your father or mother?

10. How have you been disrespectful to your parents?

Name:_____   Date:_____

Respect Effect
Word Search

```
U  Q  E  Q  S  C  R  I  P  T  U  R  E  W  O
N  A  R  M  Q  F  O  C  U  S  I  N  G  P  B
D  E  F  N  B  A  Q  N  B  C  Z  J  K  O  E
E  W  G  H  W  A  Q  J  C  A  X  Q  P  I  D
R  Q  A  U  E  T  R  H  R  R  C  H  R  U  I
S  A  P  T  R  T  W  R  E  E  V  G  A  P  E
T  A  O  R  T  I  A  P  A  D  B  F  N  T  N
A  B  L  F  Y  T  E  O  T  S  N  D  K  E  C
N  E  O  V  U  U  R  I  U  V  S  S  J  R  E
D  L  G  X  O  D  T  U  R  C  A  I  H  W  A
I  I  I  Z  D  E  T  F  E  E  L  I  N  G  S
N  E  Z  V  C  Z  Y  A  S  X  Q  A  G  G  X
G  V  E  C  F  R  I  E  N  D  S  H  I  P  Z
Q  E  V  B  N  M  Q  A  T  R  O  U  B  L  E
D  I  S  R  E  S  P  E  C  T  F  U  L  C  Q
```

Obedience	Scripture	Prank
Attitude	Focusing	Believe
Apologize	Creatures	Scared
Friendship	Trouble	Feelings
Disrespectful	Embarrassing	Understanding

Name:_____   Date:_____

Sharing Is Caring
Matching Quiz

 A.    B.    C.    D.

Match the character to his/her description. Choose one Bible verse from the box that best applies to each statement.

_____ 1. This character explains that when we are punished for our sins, it is not pleasant. Bible verse:

_____ 2. This character needs to share her room with her sister. Bible verse:

_____ 3. This character gets hurt during an argument with her sister. Bible verse:

_____ 4. This character writes a note in the girls' storybook. Bible verse:

Bible verses to choose from:
2 Timothy 2:23
Hebrews 12:11
Galatians 5:13
*Hebrews 13:16
*Memory verse

Sharing Is Caring
Discussion Questions

1. What did June and January argue about? List all that you can recall.

2. How could the girls show affection toward each other?

3. How did the girls react when they found out they would have to share a bedroom?

4. What was the reason for June and January's dad getting angry with them? How did he punish them?

5. What do you think June and January could have done better in their situation?

6. How did January treat June after she was hurt?

7. After January read her mom's letter, what did she do?

8. What is the difference between being greedy and being generous?

9. Why does punishment help us to remember not to sin again?

10. Why do sisters and brothers argue sometimes?

Name:_____ Date:_____

Sharing Is Caring
Word Search

```
Q A S O R R O W F U L U F R P
W T D H B Q W T Y M N Y O Y U
E R F V A A B L A M E T R G N
A U G G N R S Y U N F E G C I
R T H R M N I T J E A R I S S
G H J E L B D N C B I F V J H
U F K E K V C I G V R B I H M
I U L D J C F R H C N V N K E
N L O Y G I V Q J X E C G I N
G N I C R X B W K Z S D P N T
R E U C F J E S U S S S L D F
T S A X D Z F E L D C W M N S
Y S T P R A Y I N G X Q N E E
U I E Z S L O V I N G A B S R
S E R V A N T H O O D Z G S T
```

Forgiving	Sharing	Sacrifice
Jesus	Fairness	Greedy
Loving	Praying	Blame
Sorrowful	Kindness	Arguing
Servanthood	Punishment	Truthfulness

Unique Gifts
Matching Quiz

A.    B.    C.    D.

Match the character to his/her description. Choose one Bible verse from the box that best applies to each statement.

_____ 1. This character makes fun of another by calling him a baby lobster. Bible verse:

_____ 2. This character helps his new friends even though they left him out of basketball. Bible verse:

_____ 3. This character wants to include his new friend in the basketball game. Bible verse:

_____ 4. This character teaches her students that we all have strengths and weaknesses. Bible verse:

Bible verses to choose from:
Proverbs 19:29
1 Corinthians 12:17-18
Proverbs 18:24
*Hebrews 12:14
*Memory verse

Unique Gifts
Discussion Questions

1. Why did Marcus not want Carter to play ball with them?

2. What did Carter ask Jesus when he prayed to Him?

3. How did Carter help Freddy in school?

4. How did Carter help David on the way home from school?

5. What does "we are all part of one body doing different things" mean?

6. What special basketball skills did David, Carter, Freddy, and Marcus have?

7. Why do you think Marcus wanted to have Carter on his team next time?

8. Do you think Carter needed David's help for them to win?

9. What does "as each has received a gift, use it to serve one another" mean?

10. What gifts or talents do you have? How can you serve others using your gifts or talents?

Name: _____   Date: _____

Unique Gifts
Word Search

O	S	W	V	S	H	A	R	I	N	G	V	Z	P	C
Q	P	D	E	A	G	I	F	T	S	E	B	W	O	O
K	R	P	B	A	I	U	L	K	I	N	N	I	I	N
I	A	F	O	Z	K	Y	M	J	U	I	M	N	U	T
N	Y	B	N	R	O	N	N	H	Y	U	L	N	Y	R
D	E	A	R	X	T	T	E	G	T	S	K	I	S	O
N	R	C	M	E	P	U	B	S	R	Q	J	N	T	L
E	A	K	L	C	S	R	N	F	S	W	H	G	R	L
S	I	P	K	V	H	P	V	I	E	E	G	A	E	I
S	U	A	J	B	J	E	E	D	T	R	F	Q	N	N
W	Y	C	H	N	K	W	C	C	W	I	D	W	G	G
E	T	K	G	M	L	Q	X	S	T	T	E	E	T	Q
F	R	I	E	N	D	S	H	I	P	Y	S	S	H	D
T	A	L	E	N	T	A	Z	A	Q	U	A	F	T	X
R	T	H	A	N	K	F	U	L	N	E	S	S	V	Z

Gifts	Sharing	Talent
Weakness	Backpack	Winning
Strength	Prayer	Genius
Friendship	Kindness	Controlling
Respect	Opportunities	Thankfulness

SeaKids

Better Together
Matching Quiz

A.    B.    C.    D.

Match the character to his/her description. Choose one Bible verse from the box that best applies to each statement.

____ 1. This character disciplines Mandy and June for their fight on the playground. Bible verse:

____ 2. This character is jealous of Susie and June's new friendship. Bible verse:

____ 3. This character comes up with a solution to help both of her friends. Bible verse:

____ 4. This character does not invite Mandy to her birthday party. Bible verse:

Bible verses to choose from:
Luke 6:27
*Matthew 5:9
Proverbs 14:30
Matthew 5:39
*Memory verse

Better Together
Discussion Questions

1. Why do you think Susie and June are good friends?

2. How did Mandy treat June?

3. What did Mandy and June do to cause a problem for Susie?

4. What did Susie ask Jesus?

5. Is it ever good to wrestle or fight with another person? Why?

   What could June and Mandy have done differently?

6. What did Susie do to help the situation?

7. How did Mandy and June act when they saw each other at

   Susie's party?

8. How do you celebrate birthdays?

9. What does the word "sensitive" mean?

10. How is Jesus a good friend to you?

Name: _____   Date: _____

Better Together
Word Search

```
Q  G  F  S  E  N  S  I  T  I  V  E  A  Q  F
W  U  N  D  E  R  S  T  A  N  D  I  N  G  R
D  H  S  F  D  A  D  P  O  D  F  Z  E  W  I
A  A  R  G  U  I  N  G  U  S  G  P  R  U  E
I  J  N  G  S  P  B  L  Y  N  T  R  T  N  N
N  K  A  C  A  O  V  K  I  N  G  A  P  D  D
V  L  W  H  E  I  C  N  E  J  H  Y  U  E  S
I  M  E  J  Q  R  E  M  T  E  J  E  I  R  H
T  N  R  K  W  T  D  J  R  S  K  R  O  W  I
A  B  T  L  S  N  X  H  E  U  A  C  P  A  P
T  V  Y  I  A  U  Z  G  W  S  M  N  M  T  V
I  C  L  M  E  Y  A  F  Q  A  N  B  D  E  C
O  X  M  P  K  I  N  D  N  E  S  S  K  R  X
N  O  U  O  R  T  D  F  E  E  L  I  N  G  S
C  Z  I  D  E  C  O  R  A  T  I  O  N  S  Z
```

Sensitive   Dancer   Invitation

Jesus   Feelings   Prayer

Kindness   Listening   Decorations

Underwater   Understanding   Arguing

Sand   Friendship   Commandment

Cleanliness Is Next to Godliness Matching Quiz

A.    B.    C.    D.

Match the character to his/her description. Choose one Bible verse from the box that best applies to each statement.

_____ 1. This character goes to the doctor.

Bible verse:

_____ 2. This character is unorganized and does not help

around the house. Bible verse:

_____ 3. This character teases Susie about how neat her desk

is when it is empty. Bible verse:

_____ 4.This character stays with Susie to help around the house.

Bible verse:

Bible verses to choose from:
*1 Corinthians 14:40
Galatians 6:2
Psalm 147:3
Ephesians 5:4
*Memory verse

Name:_____   Date:_____

Cleanliness Is Next to Godliness Discussion Questions

1. What did Miss Sally want Susie to do that she was not doing?

2. Why did Grandma have to stay with Susie?

3. How could Susie have been a better helper for her grandmother?

4. Why did Susie think her grandmother was being unfair?

5. Why did Miss Sally take away all of Susie's things in her desk?

6. What happened to Susie right after she prayed to Jesus?

7. What happened to Susie after she handed in her homework? What

   happened when she went home?

8. Why do you think Apostle Paul wrote that things should be done

   decently and in order?

9. Are you messy sometimes? How can you be a better helper at home?

10. What would you like to ask Jesus to help you with today?

41

Name: _____   Date: _____

Cleanliness Is Next to Godliness
Word Search

```
O R G A N I Z E D U I B N J K
Q B N U I F D G R A T E F U L
R C M Y J W I S D O M V M H O
E V K T H G S A S Y U H P W V
S X J H E L P F U L I E O O E
P C H R G H Q C D A O A I R N
O A H O F J U X Q S P L U R O
N R G E M K W N W D A I Y I P
S E F C D E E Z J F S N T E E
I L D H S M W P E U D G R D R
B E S O A N R O Z G S C E G A
L S A R Z B Y O R H F T W F T
E S Q E X T H A N K F U L D I
A Z W S C V U I M N G X Q S O
P U N I S H M E N T H Z A A N
```

Grateful	Organized	Wisdom
Healing	Careless	Worried
Love	Homework	Thankful
Unjust	Responsible	Chores
Helpful	Operation	Punishment

This Is My Father's World
Matching Quiz

A.    B.    C.   D.

Match the character to his/her description. Choose one Bible verse from the box that best applies to each statement.

_____ 1. This character tells her friend that he should pick up his water bottle. Bible verse:

_____ 2. This character does not seem concerned that he litters often. Bible verse:

_____ 3. This character explains that God is the true owner of everything. Bible verse:

_____ 4. This character researches Bible verses to help her friend stop littering. Bible verse:

Bible verses to choose from:
        Psalm 37:30
        *Psalm 24:1
        Luke 21:15
        Romans 8:7
*Memory verse

This Is My Father's World
Discussion Questions

1. What did Freddy do with his water bottle? What did Melissa tell him to do with it?

2. Why do you think Freddy thought it was no big deal to let his garbage "float" away?

3. How did Freddy feel when Marcus threw garbage in his backpack, and what did Melissa say to Freddy?

4. Why did Freddy pray to Jesus?

5. Why do we have to take care of God's earth?

6. What can happen if we don't take care of God's earth?

7. What would Jesus want us to do to keep the earth cleaner?

8. Do we own anything or do we have the privilege of using what we have?

9. What kind of trash have you left behind or placed in a garbage can?

10. What does God own?

Name: _____   Date: _____

This Is My Father's World
Word Search

```
C  R  R  X  D  E  U  T  E  R  O  N  O  M  Y
O  T  E  E  Z  O  I  H  J  F  G  R  T  C  V
N  Y  W  C  S  O  M  E  R  S  A  U  L  T  B
C  L  Q  V  A  P  U  G  K  D  H  E  Y  X  S
E  I  B  A  S  K  E  T  B  A  L  L  U  Z  T
N  T  A  B  D  P  Y  C  L  S  J  W  O  A  E
T  T  G  N  S  L  T  F  A  K  Q  W  S  W
R  E  S  P  O  N  S  I  B  L  E  W  N  D  A
A  R  D  M  F  K  R  D  M  Z  L  A  E  F  R
T  I  F  L  G  H  W  S  N  X  P  E  R  G  D
E  N  G  K  H  J  E  A  B  C  O  R  I  T  S
S  G  H  J  C  R  E  A  T  I  O  N  O  H  H
G  A  R  B  A  G  E  Q  V  V  I  T  P  J  I
P  U  P  R  A  C  T  I  C  E  U  Y  L  K  P
O  I  F  A  I  T  H  F  U  L  N  E  S  S  N
```

Respect	Somersault	Earth
Faithfulness	Basketball	Littering
Creation	Practice	Responsible
Owner	Garbage	Heaven
Stewardship	Deuteronomy	Concentrates

45

Too Much Screen Time
Matching Quiz

A.    B.    C.    D.

Match the character to his/her description. Choose one Bible verse from the box that best applies to each statement.

_____ 1. This character explains that God made our world beautiful to enjoy outside. Bible verse:

_____ 2. This character is having trouble letting go of his video game. Bible verse:

_____ 3. This character causes Carter to have great fear. Bible verse:

_____ 4. This character is distracted by Carter's video game on the playground. Bible verse:

Bible verses to choose from:
Psalm 119:37
*Psalm 56:3
Zechariah 8:5
1 Peter 1:14-15
*Memory verse

Name:_____   Date: _____

Too Much Screen Time
Discussion Questions

1. Why do you think Carter liked playing video games?

2. What makes you think Carter was addicted to his video game?

3. What did Carter's mother ask him to do and why did Carter's mother say "Snap out of it?"

4. What bothered Carter when he went outside to play with the boys?

5. What happened that caused Carter to not want to play his game?

6. What did Carter pray to Jesus about?

7. What video games do you play?

8. What can you do outside that you can't do while playing a video game?

9. Why does Jesus like to see boys and girls playing outside?

10. Do you know the difference between what is make-believe and what is real?

Name:_____   Date:_____

Too Much Screen Time
Word Search

```
Q G F L K I N C R E D I B L E
W A T C H I N G J A W S Z S A
B H D P J J H Q K Z A D X D V
A A T S G K G W C X C U G F A
Z J R E H Z E C H A R I A H L
F K A R F L D E E T E L M G I
R L Q P A M S R A Y A K I H A
I M W E D C A T T U T J N J N
E N E N S N U Y E N I E G K T
N B R T A B Q D R H O S V L L
D V T O Z V W U A F N Y C B Y
S C R E E N E I L C H O R E S
H C W O R T H L E S S H B N Q
I X Y F I L T H Y S F G N M W
P Z U I X C R G R U E S O M E
```

Filthy	Valiantly	Gruesome
Friendship	Serpent	Screen
Zechariah	Creation	Gaming
Incredible	Cheater	Chores
Barracuda	Watching	Worthless

48

SeaKids

A Thankful Heart
Matching Quiz

A.    B.    C.    D.

Match the character to his/her description. Choose one Bible verse from the box that best applies to each statement.

_____1. This character complains about many things but learns

to be thankful. Bible verse:

_____2. This character leaves a note on Mandy's lunchbox.

Bible verse:

_____3. This character is thankful for everything she has.

Bible verse:

_____4.This character does not like to waste food.

Bible verse:

Bible verses to choose from:
      *1 Thessalonians 5:18
          John 6:12
         Hebrews 13:5
         1 Timothy 4:4
*Memory verse

Name:_____   Date:_____

A Thankful Heart
Discussion Questions

1. What did Mandy complain about?

2. Why did Melissa want Mandy's sandwich?

3. Mandy's mother left a note on Mandy's lunchbox. What did it say?

4. Why did Mandy think that no one seemed to care about her problems?

5. What did Mandy ask for when she prayed to Jesus?

6. What do you think Mandy should have prayed for?

7. Why was Melissa so happy?

8. When Melissa prayed to Jesus, what did she ask for?

9. How was Melissa a good influence on Mandy?

10. Is it the things we have that make us happy? What makes you happy?

Name:_____   Date: _____

A Thankful Heart
Word Search

```
C D S W E A T B A N D S V R T
Q O A I Z F D C R E A T I O N
W F R M X J E T P A C K B E Q
E J Z I C G S H F U I C N W W
R E X S N H A R E D E E M E R
T S C T N T Z J D Y O X M Q E
Y U V A Q K H A P P I N E S S
U S G K W L X I S T P Z L C R
I G B E E P C K A R L A K H T
O H N Y R O V L A N K Q J O B
T H A N K F U L N E S S H O I
P J M T T I S E E D S D G L K
G K Q R Y U B M Q E J F F A E
O R E J E C T E D W H G D S Y
D L W E C O M P L A I N I N G
```

God	Jesus	Bike
Happiness	Sweatbands	Jetpack
Mistake	School	Seeds
Creation	Rejected	Redeemer
Corinthians	Thankfulness	Complaining

Love Is the Best Policy
Matching Quiz

A.  B.  C.  D.

Match the character to his/her description. Choose one Bible verse from the box that best applies to each statement.

_____ 1. This character tells her class, "The truth will set you free." Bible verse:

_____ 2. This character learns that the truth needs to be given with love. Bible verse:

_____ 3. This character is offended when Susie makes fun of his game. Bible verse:

_____ 4. This character tells that Susie she needs to express herself with more love. Bible verse:

Bible verses to choose from:
Proverbs 19:11
*1 John 3:18
Ephesians 4:15
John 8:32
*Memory verse

52

Love Is the Best Policy
Discussion Questions

1. What did Susie complain about to her father regarding her lunch?

   Was she being nice to him?

2. Why does Miss Sally think people don't like to hear the truth?

3. What did Susie's grandmother say to Susie that made Susie sad?

4. How did Susie learn to use her words when telling the truth?

5. Do you think Susie was ungrateful or just truthful in telling her father

   that she did not like her dinner?

6. Why is telling the truth a good thing to do?

7. How can you hurt someone's feelings with the truth?

8. What truth was Jesus talking about when He said to tell the truth?

9. What does it mean to tell the truth in love?

10. When you don't like something, how do you tell the other person

    you don't like it?

Love Is the Best Policy
Word Search

Name: _____ Date: _____

```
H  G  G  O  O  D  N  E  S  S  K  Z  X  T  R
Q  O  H  G  H  Q  A  V  C  L  J  A  H  Y  E
C  O  M  M  A  N  D  M  E  N  T  D  E  P  Q
W  F  J  E  P  A  T  I  E  N  C  E  A  O  F
T  D  K  F  W  W  S  B  X  P  Q  F  V  I  A
H  S  L  D  J  O  D  N  A  O  W  B  E  Y  I
A  D  I  N  N  E  R  M  Z  T  R  I  N  T  T
N  A  M  S  K  E  F  K  Q  R  T  R  C  R  H
K  P  D  E  L  I  C  I  O  U  S  T  V  E  F
F  O  N  A  L  L  G  N  W  T  Y  H  B  S  U
U  I  B  Z  U  R  H  D  E  H  U  D  N  D  L
L  U  V  F  P  T  J  N  R  F  O  A  M  F  N
E  Y  Y  X  O  Y  K  E  T  U  K  Y  K  G  E
R  O  S  H  A  R  K  S  Y  L  J  G  J  H  S
J  T  V  C  I  U  L  S  U  I  H  S  I  N  S
```

Sharks	Delicious	Sins
Thankful	Truthful	Birthday
Patience	Homework	Joyful
Kindness	Heaven	Dinner
Goodness	Commandment	Faithfulness

54

Name:_____   Date: _____

Bible Challenge
Matching Quiz

A.    B.    C.    D.

Match the character to his/her description. Choose one Bible verse from the box that best applies to each statement.

_____ 1. This character gives her class a Bible quiz.

Bible verse:

_____ 2. This character wants to read his comic book more

than his Bible. Bible verse:

_____ 3. This character wins the Bible quiz and gets a reward.

Bible verse:

_____ 4. This character asks David about the fifth commandment

on the playground. Bible verse:

Bible verses to choose from:
Matthew 6:33
Philippians 3:14
*Exodus 20:12
2 Timothy 3:16
*Memory verse

Bible Challenge
Discussion Questions

1. Why was David excited to receive something in the mail?

2. Why did David take the quiz from his teacher's desk?

3. Why was David embarrassed when he answered the questions in class?

4. What did David do after he confessed to his teacher that he cheated?

5. What did David do to help him remember what he read in his Bible?

6. Why is it important to know God's Word?

7. What do you do to help remember what Jesus said in the Bible?

8. Do you spend more time on other things than you do reading your

   Bible? If you do, what are these other things?

9. Why do you think it makes Jesus happy to read His Word?

10. How do you help yourself remember what you read in your Bible?

Bible Challenge
Word Search

```
C H E A T I N G Y X C Q U I Z
Q S D H G J H T U Z V C F O A
W W I N N E R R I A B O G I S
V D S J F K G E O S N N G R Z
E F A K R E P E N T I F H U X
R G P M D L F W P D M U J L C
S H P N S P D Q N D P S K E V
E C O M I C S A L M O E L S B
S J I B A O T M K E I D M U C
E K N V Q S S N J M U D N Y O
R L T C R I I B H O N O R T N
T P E E W U A N H R Y S B R T
Y O D X E Y Z V S I T A V E E
U N A Z R T X C G Z R Q C W S
U I T R E A S U R E E W X Q T
```

Quiz	Comics	Sins
Honor	Verses	Winner
Cheating	Memorize	Contest
Repent	Treasure	Confused
Rules	Understanding	Disappointed

The New Babysitter Matching Quiz

A.    B.    C.    D.

Match the character to his/her description. Choose one Bible verse from the box that best applies to each statement.

_____ 1. This character gets a full-time job and can no longer babysit the boys. Bible verse:

_____ 2. This character wants to behave badly so the new babysitter will not come back. Bible verse:

_____ 3. This character reluctantly joins his friend in misbehaving. Bible verse:

_____ 4. This character shows kindness to the boys even though they were not nice. Bible verse:

Bible verses to choose from:
Leviticus 19:18
2 Thessalonians 3:10
James 4:17
*Proverbs 11:17
*Memory verse

Name:_____   Date:_____

The New Babysitter
Discussion Questions

1. Why was David sad that Fritz could no longer be his babysitter?

2. What did David say about the new babysitter before he met her?

3. How did David treat his new babysitter, Sarah?

4. How did Sarah treat the boys?

5. What did the boys do after they realized they treated Sarah badly?

6. Why do you think Sarah came back to babysit again?

7. What fun things do you do when you have a babysitter?

8. How do you treat a new babysitter or a new friend?

9. What do you know about the Fruit of the Spirit?

10. What is your favorite Fruit of the Spirit? Why?

The New Babysitter
Word Search

B	F	L	G	O	O	D	N	E	S	S	R	T	Q	D
Q	A	K	L	K	J	H	L	K	A	D	E	Y	P	I
W	I	B	M	J	K	J	E	S	U	S	W	U	I	S
E	T	J	Y	H	H	O	M	E	W	O	R	K	G	R
R	H	H	N	S	L	G	M	J	Q	F	Q	O	G	E
T	F	G	B	G	I	F	F	R	U	I	T	P	Y	S
P	U	F	E	F	P	T	N	P	W	G	Z	L	B	P
E	L	D	H	D	J	D	T	O	E	H	X	K	A	E
A	N	S	A	S	O	O	B	E	R	J	C	J	C	C
C	E	A	V	A	I	S	Y	I	R	K	V	H	K	T
E	S	Z	I	Q	U	A	V	U	L	O	V	E	V	F
Y	S	X	O	W	S	P	I	R	I	T	B	F	C	U
U	P	C	R	E	Y	Z	C	Y	T	L	N	S	X	L
I	O	V	B	R	T	X	K	I	N	D	N	E	S	S
C	R	U	S	T	A	C	E	A	N	S	M	A	Z	B

Fruit	Peace	Jesus
Behavior	Faithfulness	Babysitter
Homework	Goodness	Piggyback
Kindness	Joy	Spirit
Disrespectful	Love	Crustaceans

Name:_____   Date: _____

Church Is for Everyone!
Matching Quiz

A.    B.    C.    D.

Match the character to his/her description. Choose one Bible verse from the box that best applies to each statement.

_____ 1. This character wants to play baseball instead of going to church. Bible verse:

_____ 2. This character loves singing praise songs, especially with Snappy Cat Starfish. Bible verse:

_____ 3. This character does not know what the pastor is talking about during church service. Bible verse:

_____ 4. This character tells his son that he has an invitation from the most powerful being in the universe. Bible verse:

Bible verses to choose from:
Psalm 150:6
Hebrews 10:25
*Peter 1:15
John 14:26
*Memory verse

61

Church Is for Everyone!
Discussion Questions

1. What reasons did Christian give about not wanting to go to church?

    What did he do instead?

2. What happened to Christian when he got hit in the head with the ball?

3. What is your favorite Bible story about Jesus?

4. How do you praise Jesus?

5. What do you talk to Jesus about?

6. What is your favorite part of church service? Why?

7. Who is your favorite singer? Why?

8. Why is Jesus a superhero?

9. How do you pray to Jesus?

10. How does going to church make you feel?

Church Is for Everyone!
Word Search

```
B A R R A C U D A C F C X D F
Q D S E R H J D F I Q A V S N
W F A F T U S S G M W K I P A
E G Z R Y R K C H P E J Z R Z
R H T I U C L A A O R G B A A
T J I E I H P Q J R G S N I R
S K X N A G O W K T E A M S E
U L C D V C I E L A Z D P I T
P P V S B I H R M N X P O N H
E O B H N F T I N T C L I G G
R I N I M D U A N V V K U A H
H U M P A S Y T T G J E S U S
E P O W E R F U L I N J Y Q J
R Y Q W B I B L E B O Y T W K
O T S T A R F I S H Q N R E V
```

Teaching	Church	Fair
Barracuda	Nazareth	Invitation
Scared	Bible	Jesus
Starfish	Important	Powerful
Praising	Friendship	Superhero

63

Name:_____   Date:_____

Praying for Puppy
Matching Quiz

A.    B.    C.    D.

Match the character to his/her description. Choose one Bible verse from the box that best applies to each statement.

_____ 1. This character asks Susie if she thinks she is responsible

enough for a pet. Bible verse:

_____ 2. This character learns a lesson in responsibility.

Bible verse:

_____ 3. This character warns Susie not to leave Tails alone at

the playground. Bible verse:

_____ 4. This character reminds Susie that she is working for Jesus.

Bible verse:

Bible verses to choose from:
*Proverbs 8:33
Colossians 3:23
Psalm 37:30
Proverbs 13:16
*Memory verse

Praying for Puppy
Discussion Questions

1. How was Susie irresponsible and disobedient when she took her puppy to the park?

2. How did Susie's parents react when they found out Susie lost her puppy? How did they extend grace to Susie?

3. What did Susie and her mother do to help find the puppy?

4. What did Susie ask Jesus in prayer?

5. How did Jesus answer Susie's prayer?

6. What are some of the things you have wanted for your birthday?

7. Why are birthdays special?

8. What chores or responsibilities do you have at home?

9. What have you asked Jesus for lately?

10. How has Jesus used you or your parents in answering prayers for other people?

Praying for Puppy
Word Search

```
Q  Z  X  P  L  G  R  A  C  I  O  U  S  X  F
R  E  S  P  O  N  S  I  B  L  E  E  R  F  O
W  A  C  O  K  L  Q  H  P  B  V  W  T  O  R
P  S  V  B  J  P  W  J  G  R  C  Q  Y  U  G
U  D  B  I  H  O  E  S  F  N  O  L  U  N  I
P  F  N  R  G  S  R  A  D  M  X  M  I  D  V
P  G  M  T  F  T  F  S  L  Z  K  I  A  E
Y  H  Q  H  D  E  Y  E  A  M  O  J  P  S  N
E  J  W  D  S  R  U  T  Z  N  A  S  L  Z  E
C  K  E  A  A  M  I  Y  X  B  S  H  T  S  S
R  R  R  Y  Z  H  O  P  E  F  U  L  K  D  S
T  L  Y  I  X  N  O  K  C  V  D  G  J  F  Z
Y  P  T  I  C  P  R  O  T  E  C  T  E  D  X
U  O  Y  U  N  B  P  L  P  R  A  Y  I  N  G
I  P  L  A  Y  G  R  O  U  N  D  F  H  G  C
```

Poster	Lost	Found
Safety	Birthday	Promise
Gracious	Puppy	Crying
Hopeful	Protected	Praying
Forgiveness	Responsible	Playground

Practice Makes Pretty Perfect
Matching Quiz

A.    B.    C.    D.

Match the character to his/her description. Choose one Bible verse from the box that best applies to each statement.

_____ 1. This character encourages his swim team to practice for their race. Bible verse:

_____ 2. This character does not think she needs to practice or study for math. Bible verse:

_____ 3. This character cheers on Mandy and Susie at the race with Melissa. Bible verse:

_____ 4. This character gets extra practice and wins first place in the final race. Bible verse:

Bible verses to choose from:
James 1:4
1 Thessalonians 2:11
1 Corinthians 9:24
*Proverbs 14:23
*Memory verse

Practice Makes Pretty Perfect
Discussion Questions

1. Why did Mandy think she did not need to stay for swim practice?

2. Why did Mandy think she did not need to study for her math test?

3. Do you think Mandy was bragging or just confident? What is the difference between the two?

4. What happened to Mandy when she took the math test?

5. How did Mandy do in the race? How did she feel after?

6. How did Mandy's friends treat her when they lost the race?

7. What does it mean for someone to be "gifted?"

8. What gift or talent do you think the Lord has given to you?

9. How do you use your gift or talent to help others?

10. How do you practice to make your gift or talent better?

Name:_____   Date:_____

Practice Makes Pretty Perfect
Word Search

```
C O M P E T I T I O N B Q S S
Q F D I P E R F E C T I O N A
E G H U L N M B N P L V O D Z
M H O Y R A C E M C K I W P X
B J M T K B L V Q H T R E R C
A T E A M W O R K A J E R A C
R K W R J V K C L M H P T C O
R L O E H C J U W P G R Y T N
A O R W G X T X E I F E U I F
S I K Q F A H Z R O D S I C I
S U S B R A G G I N G E O E D
E Y A G D Z G A T S S N P F E
D T N X S A F S Y H Z T L G N
W O Z T A L E N T I X C K H C
C R T E S T S D U P R A Y J E
```

Tests	Pray	Race
Talent	Represent	Practice
Confidence	Teamwork	Homework
Competition	Embarrassed	Bragging
Championship	Perfection	Congratulations

SeaKids

Friends First
Matching Quiz

A.    B.    C.    D.

Match the character to his/her description. Choose one Bible verse from the box that best applies to each statement.

_____ 1. This character will not share her new toy.

Bible verse:

_____ 2. This character accidentally breaks a toy that is not hers and tells the truth. Bible verse:

_____ 3. This character hides the truth from her friend.

Bible verse:

_____ 4. This character quotes Apostle Paul about being content.

Bible verse:

Bible verses to choose from:
Psalm 34:13
*1 John 3:18
Philippians 4:11-13
Hebrews 13:16
*Memory verse

Friends First
Discussion Questions

1. Why was Melissa saving her money?

2. How do you think Melissa earned her money?

3. What did Melissa do when Susie broke Mandy's toy?

4. Why do you think Melissa should have told Mandy that her toy broke?

5. How did Melissa try to make things right with Mandy?

6. How does it make you feel when someone doesn't share with you?

7. How can you share with others?

8. Do you think it is better to earn money to buy a toy or to have it just

    given to you? Why?

9. How do you think Jesus feels when we are deceitful? Why does

    He feel that way?

10. How can you be kind to your family or your friends?

Friends First
Word Search

```
A C C I D E N T A L L Y A X C
Q O R Z A P O L O G I Z E C O
F I E X Q W Z A Y T D S Q V N
R U S F A S O M E R S A U L T
I S P O S E X S U R F G W B E
E H E R D S E L F I S H E B N
N A C G F R C D I E D H R R T
D R T I G T V P O W E J T O M
S I F V H T O F A Q C K Y K E
H N U E J Y B Y P T E L U E N
I G L C K U N G S Z I M I N T
P Y N V M O N E Y X T E O N A
W T E B L I M H L C F N N M D
E R S N M O P J K V U B P C F
R E S P O N S I B I L I T Y E
```

Selfish	Toys	Broken
Accidentally	Patience	Deceitful
Forgive	Money	Sharing
Somersault	Friendship	Apologize
Responsibility	Contentment	Respectfulness

Name:_____   Date:_____

Safety First
Matching Quiz

A.    B.    C.    D.

Match the character to his/her description. Choose one Bible verse from the box that best applies to each statement.

_____ 1. This character is thankful for her friends' hard work.

Bible verse:

_____ 2. This character teaches her son a lesson about safety.

Bible verse:

_____ 3. This character helps David rebuild their friend's go-kart.

Bible verse:

_____ 4. This character learns that safety is always important.

Bible verse:

Bible verses to choose from:
Proverbs 11:14
Romans 12:10-11
*Proverbs 27:12
Philippians 2:4
*Memory verse

Safety First
Discussion Questions

1. What were Freddy and David building? Why were they building it?

2. What rules did David's mother give David?

3. What happened when David didn't follow the rules?

4. How could the outcome have been worse than it was?

5. At first David did not want to fix Mandy's go-kart. Why did he end up fixing it?

6. How did David and Freddy make Mandy's go-kart better than it originally was?

7. What lesson did David and Freddy learn about obedience and sacrifice?

8. What have you made or helped to make with your friend or parent?

9. Why does Jesus want us to obey our parents?

10. What can happen if you don't obey your parents? How do you think it makes Jesus feel when you don't obey?

Safety First
Word Search

```
L W Z X L R A C E V L K O P D
O E D I S O B E Y E D J I R I
R R A C P K M Q B C P H U O N
D T S V O J N R U L E S Y T J
Q S A C R I F I C E O G T E U
M Y D B I H B W N X I F R C R
O H F F U G C E W Z U D E T E
U E G N A F V O M H Y S W I D
T L H M Y S C R R A E A Q O J
H M J L T D T T P A T E M N K
G E K H O S P I T A L Z L Z M
U T L Q R S X Y O Q R H N S N
A U D E S T R O Y E D X O X B
R I P W E A Z U I W E C V O V
D O F R I E N D S H I P B C D
```

Fast	Lord	Race
Hospital	Coralhood	Wheels
Sacrifice	Helmet	Rules
Destroyed	Protection	Injured
Friendship	Mouthguard	Disobeyed

Name:_____ Date:_____

Grudge or Grace
Matching Quiz

A.  B.  C.  D.

Match the character to his/her description. Choose one Bible verse from the box that best applies to each statement.

_____ 1. This character teaches the class the Ten Commandments.

Bible verse:

_____ 2. This character holds a grudge against everyone.

Bible verse:

_____ 3. This character tells June not to hold onto her anger.

Bible verse:

_____ 4. This character knows the second commandment.

Bible verse:

Bible verses to choose from:
*Psalm 119:11
Ephesians 4:31
John 14:15
Leviticus 19:18
*Memory verse

Grudge or Grace
Discussion Questions

1. Why was June angry?

2. What did June decide to do after she complained to Jesus?

3. What did June pray to Jesus about at the end of the story?

4. What are the two most important commandments?

5. Why do you think God gave us the Ten Commandments?

6. How do you act toward others when you are angry?

7. How do you think Jesus wants you to act when you are angry at someone?

8. How do you treat others nicely?

9. When someone is holding a grudge against you, how can you show them God's grace?

10. Do you pray to Jesus when you are angry? How do you feel after you pray to Him?

Grudge or Grace
Word Search

```
Q E M B A R R A S S I N G U U
T Z A N G E R P K E Q A Z Y N
W E H B I T T E R N E S S T D
C X N G X C O M J S W S X T E
O C E D Z G I N H I E P C O R
M V I F E V R B G T R R V G S
M B G D P R U A F I T A B E T
A A H S O B H V C V Y Y N T A
N L B A I N Y E D E U E M H N
D O O W U M T C A P I R K E D
M N R E Y Q R X S R O D J R I
E E J G R U D G E K T F H A N
N N K R T W E Z A J H E G S G
T M L I S T E N I N G G D D X
S L F O R G I V E N E S S F C
```

Grudge	Alone	Grace
Anger	Together	Embarrassing
Listening	Bitterness	Prayer
Sensitive	Forgiveness	Neighbor
Commandments	Tenderhearted	Understanding

Faith Over Fear
Matching Quiz

A.  B.  C.  D.

Match the character to his/her description. Choose one Bible verse from the box that best applies to each statement.

_____ 1. This character is afraid to join karate and climb

the rope. Bible verse:

_____ 2. This character works hard to teach the kids karate.

Bible verse:

_____ 3. This character says karate is not about fighting, it is

about building character. Bible verse:

_____ 4. This character tells Carter that "Goliaths" are meant to

be beaten. Bible verse:

Bible verses to choose from:
Romans 5:4
Joshua 1:9
1 Samuel 17:45
*2 Timothy 1:7
*Memory verse

Faith Over Fear
Discussion Questions

1. What did Christian say about karate class?

2. Why did Carter not want to climb the rope to ring the bell?

3. What did Christian say he did to overcome his fear of joining the karate club?

4. Why do you think Carter was happy that he made it all the way through karate class?

5. What did Carter do before he tried to climb the rope to ring the bell?

6. What did Carter's friends do while he was climbing the rope? How did Carter feel when he made it to the top?

7. Why do you think it is good to be strong and courageous?

8. How do you think David felt when he faced Goliath?

9. What can you do to help yourself be brave when you are faced with fear?

10. What activities are you afraid of trying? Why are you afraid?

Name: _____   Date: _____

Faith Over Fear
Word Search

```
I  T  E  C  D  I  S  C  I  P  L  I  N  E  P
M  C  Y  M  V  Y  T  H  G  O  L  L  P  L  O
P  H  U  X  B  T  E  R  R  I  F  Y  I  N  G
R  A  J  Z  I  A  R  J  F  I  K  M  O  M  I
E  R  E  A  B  U  R  K  D  E  F  E  N  S  E
S  A  S  S  L  G  W  R  D  Y  J  N  I  B  Y
S  C  U  D  E  O  E  M  A  T  H  B  U  V  R
I  T  S  G  B  A  Q  F  S  S  G  V  Y  C  O
V  E  I  F  N  L  A  N  E  R  S  C  T  X  P
E  R  O  H  M  S  S  B  A  A  F  M  R  Z  E
Q  R  P  J  L  I  Z  V  Q  E  R  X  E  S  T
C  O  N  G  R  A  T  U  L  A  T  I  O  N  S
F  R  I  G  H  T  E  N  E  D  D  Z  E  A  T
W  E  L  K  P  O  X  C  W  K  A  R  A  T  E
F  A  I  T  H  F  U  L  N  E  S  S  W  Q  R
```

Goals	Fear	Jesus
Defense	Faithfulness	Frightened
Character	Impressive	Discipline
Karate	Bible	Rope
Terrifying	Congratulations	Embarrassment

81

The Color of Attention
Matching Quiz

A.    B.    C.    D.

Match the character to his/her description. Choose one Bible verse from the box that best applies to each statement.

_____ 1. This character does not listen to her teacher's

instructions. Bible verse:

_____ 2. This character says Melissa should learn from her mistakes.

Bible verse:

_____ 3. This character tries to help Melissa on the playground.

Bible verse:

_____ 4. This character explains the importance of paying

attention to Melissa before she leaves for school.

Bible verse:

Bible verses to choose from:
        Galatians 6:9
        Proverbs 4:25
        Proverbs 2:11
        *Proverbs 3:1
*Memory verse

82

The Color of Attention
Discussion Questions

1. Why was Melissa stained purple?

2. What was Melissa doing on the playground after being warned

   not to do it?

3. What happened to Melissa when she went to the bathroom?

4. What did Melissa pray to Jesus about?

5. What lesson did Melissa learn about not paying attention?

6. What does "gaining understanding and knowledge" mean?

7. What famous book gives us all the knowledge we need? What have

   you learned from that famous book?

8. What can cause you to not pay attention when the teacher

   is teaching class?

9. Why do you think it is important to listen and obey rules?

10. How can you learn from your mistakes?

The Color of Attention
Word Search

```
U Z X M A R K E R S X Y U C Q
N A S C X N Q I O Z C T I V W
D I R E C T I O N S C H M B E
E Q D V Z B W U P A V R O N E
R W D I S C I P L I N E N O R
S E F B A V T Y L S B E B M L
T R N E G L E C T D N W V O J
A T G N Q C A T K J M Q C B A
N Y H M W X C R J E L A X E N
D U J S E A H O R S E S Z D I
I I P R A Y E R H U K D A I T
N O K L E Z R E G S J F S E O
G P T E C H N O L O G Y D N R
A T T E N T I O N F H G F C H
Q W E C O N S E Q U E N C E S
```

Neglect	School	Markers
Discipline	Teacher	Seahorse
Prayer	Obedience	Janitor
Technology	Attention	Directions
Jesus	Understanding	Consequences

Name:_____   Date: _____

Once Lost, Now Found
Matching Quiz

A.    B.    C.    D.

Match the character to his/her description. Choose one Bible verse from the box that best applies to each statement.

_____ 1. This character loses his ball and takes his friend's

ball as his own. Bible verse:

_____ 2. This character tells David that Jesus loves when we

tell the truth. Bible verse:

_____ 3. This character finds his friend's ball and returns it.

Bible verse:

_____ 4. This character tells David to pray to Jesus when he

is sad or confused. Bible verse:

Bible verses to choose from:
3 John 1:11
*3 John 1:4
Leviticus 19:11
Jeremiah 29:12
*Memory verse

Once Lost, Now Found
Discussion Questions

1. Why do you think David decided to keep Christian's ball for himself?

2. What happened when David prayed to Jesus for guidance?

3. What did Christian do when he found David's ball?

4. How did Christian react when David told him he took Christian's ball for himself?

5. What advice did David's mom give him?

6. Why is it right that Christian forgave David?

7. What Bible verse would you give to David to help him?

8. What special talents or gifts from God do you have?

9. What does Deuteronomy 5:33 mean to you?

10. What is the first thing you should do when you are about to commit a sin?

Once Lost, Now Found
Word Search

```
T  G  B  Y  U  I  C  O  N  F  U  S  E  D  S
A  D  X  C  L  S  Q  A  D  G  H  E  L  K  U
F  A  E  N  I  U  T  R  U  S  T  L  A  S  P
A  Z  D  U  S  X  C  E  V  B  L  F  P  X  E
I  X  L  A  T  B  P  N  A  M  Y  I  O  L  R
T  R  Y  B  E  E  H  R  R  L  V  S  I  P  S
H  T  I  T  N  Q  R  H  O  E  I  H  U  L  T
F  Y  N  R  I  W  G  O  Y  M  B  N  Y  K  A
U  U  G  E  N  T  F  N  N  W  I  N  G  J  R
L  O  E  F  G  R  D  M  I  O  V  S  T  H  B
U  B  A  E  Y  U  S  K  O  Q  M  M  E  B  C
G  P  R  A  C  T  I  C  E  A  C  Y  R  A  Z
T  M  S  R  T  H  A  L  P  Z  X  Q  E  L  A
U  L  R  T  Y  U  O  J  E  S  U  S  W  L  S
O  C  O  M  M  A  N  D  M  E  N  T  S  F  D
```

Selfish	Superstar	Confused
Deuteronomy	Practice	Jesus
Ball	Lying	Trust
Listening	Faithful	Truth
Stealing	Commandments	Promise

The Worrier
Matching Quiz

A.    B.    C.    D.

Match the character to his/her description. Choose one Bible
verse from the box that best applies to each statement.

_____ 1. This character cannot stop worrying about the

tournament. Bible verse:

_____ 2. This character is worried about his coach and prays

to Jesus for help. Bible verse:

_____ 3. This character is always kind and gives compliments.

Bible verse:

_____ 4.This character teaches her son not to be anxious.

Bible verse:

Bible verses to choose from:
Matthew 7:7
1 Peter 5:7
Philippians 4:16
*Proverbs 15:1
*Memory verse

Name:_____   Date: _____

The Worrier
Discussion Questions

1. Why was Coach Crab worried?

2. What did Miss Sally and the students do to help Coach Crab?

3. What do you think your parents or teachers worry about?

4. What do you worry about?

5. When people worry, what should they do?

6. How can you help someone when they are afraid or worried?

7. How did Jesus comfort His disciples when they were worried?

8. How can teamwork be important?

9. Even if you have faith in Jesus, can you still worry about things?

10. How does the Holy Spirit help us when we are afraid or worried?

The Worrier
Word Search

```
Q R E S P O N S I B I L I T Y
W Z X P L Q W M N P O I R O N
R E Q U E S T S B P I G T U B
E A C O K M H P V R U H Y R V
R A N X I O U S C A Y T U N C
S S V I J N N O X Y T N I A X
T U B U H B D C Z E R I O M Z
Y D P Y G V E C A R E N P E T
U F N P F C R E S L W G L N E
I G M T O X E R D K Q R K T A
O H Q R D R R I F L A G S A M
S T U D E N T S F J G E J S W
C O A C H Z T I G F A I T H O
L J W E S A Y U V H D W H D R
K C H A L L E N G E S Q G F K
```

Flags	Coach	Faith
Teamwork	Students	Supportive
Thunder	Prayer	Requests
Lightning	Anxious	Soccer
Challenges	Responsibility	Tournament

90

Stop and Smell the Patience
Matching Quiz

A.    B.    C.    D.

Match the character to his/her description. Choose one Bible verse from the box that best applies to each statement.

_____ 1. This character has trouble waiting and learns a tough

lesson about patience. Bible verse:

_____ 2. This character argues with Christian about cutting the

line before school. Bible verse:

_____ 3. This character tells Christian his sister is too young to

be left behind. Bible verse:

_____ 4. This character is left alone after school and stays

with the teacher. Bible verse:

Bible verses to choose from:
1 Thessalonians 2:7
*Ephesians 4:2
Philippians 2:14
Proverbs 2:11
*Memory verse

Stop and Smell the Patience Discussion Questions

1. How was Christian not being nice to his sister?

2. How was Christian not being nice to his friends?

3. Why did Christian come home alone without his sister?

4. How do you think Mary felt when she found out Christian left school without her?

5. How do you think Christian's father felt knowing Mary was lost?

6. What did Christian say to Jesus when he prayed to Him?

7. What could have happened to Mary?

8. What causes you to be in a hurry?

9. Why do you think Jesus wants us to put the needs of others before our own needs?

10. How can you put the needs of others before your own needs?

Stop and Smell the Patience
Word Search

```
I  H  D  I  S  O  B  E  D  I  E  N  T  D  Q
R  J  G  G  F  Z  X  R  E  X  Z  D  E  F  D
R  K  A  R  R  O  G  A  N  T  Q  F  A  G  A
E  L  F  H  D  B  R  O  T  H  E  R  M  H  N
S  P  R  J  A  I  S  T  W  C  W  G  W  J  G
P  O  A  K  P  U  E  Y  Q  V  E  H  O  K  E
O  I  I  L  O  Y  L  U  A  B  R  J  R  M  R
N  U  D  M  L  T  F  I  S  N  A  K  K  N  O
S  Y  F  N  O  R  I  O  D  M  T  N  S  B  U
I  I  D  B  G  E  S  P  F  L  Y  L  G  V  S
B  T  S  V  I  W  H  M  I  S  T  A  K  E  W
L  R  S  T  Z  Q  C  M  G  K  U  P  A  C  R
E  E  A  C  E  A  P  A  T  I  E  N  C  E  E
Q  W  Z  X  S  R  V  N  H  J  I  O  Z  X  R
S  A  F  E  T  Y  B  H  U  M  I  L  I  T  Y
```

Mistake	Anger	Brother
Apologize	Patience	Selfish
Safety	Sister	Afraid
Humility	Arrogant	Teamwork
Disobedient	Irresponsible	Dangerous

Let Others Shine
Matching Quiz

A.    B.    C.    D.

Match the character to his/her description. Choose one Bible verse from the box that best applies to each statement.

_____ 1. This character tells Freddy that God opposes the proud.

Bible verse:

_____ 2. This character learns the importance of his role as

John the Baptist. Bible verse:

_____ 3. This character is in charge of the school play.

Bible verse:

_____ 4. This character is afraid to take the lead role and

prays with his friends. Bible verse:

Bible verses to choose from:
Matthew 25:21
*Matthew 18:20
James 4:6
Luke 7:28
*Memory verse

Let Others Shine
Discussion Questions

1. How did Freddy feel about his acting ability?

2. How did Carter feel about his acting ability?

3. Why did everyone laugh at Freddy? How did it make him feel?

4. What did Carter say to make Freddy feel better?

5. How did Freddy feel about not getting the lead role in the play?

   What did he say about it?

6. What did Freddy say when Miss Sally announced that Carter would

   take the lead role because Ben was sick?

7. What did Freddy's mother tell Freddy about his role of being John

   the Baptist?

8. What did Freddy and Carter do before they went on stage?

9. When you pray to Jesus, how does He answer your prayers?

10. How do you point others to Jesus?

Let Others Shine
Word Search

```
S E L F I S H N E S S B V R T
Q S A Y T L Z A U D I T I O N
C D M E M O R I Z E F A C E Y
W H Z U R K X E X G D L X W C
E F A I S J C R C P S E Z Q O
J G U R E T V T V E A N D S S
E H D O A H A Y B R Q T S P T
S J I P P C B G N F W S F O U
U K E M R G T U E O E N G T M
S L N N O F N E M R R M H L E
R P C B U D M I R M T P J I Q
T O E V D S Q O L H Y O K G W
Y I X C W A W P K J U I L H E
U R E S P O N S I B I L I T Y
A C T O R Q E N E R V O U S R
```

Actor	Stage	Jesus
Perform	Nervous	Audience
Talents	Memorize	Character
Proud	Audition	Costume
Spotlight	Responsibility	Selfishness

Knowledge Is the Best Treasure
Matching Quiz

A.    B.    C.    D.

Match the character to his/her description. Choose one Bible verse from the box that best applies to each statement.

_____ 1. This character says he knows more than the others

ever will. Bible verse:

_____ 2. This character is tricked into eating a spicy plant.

Bible verse:

_____ 3. This character teaches the class about the Golden Rule.

Bible verse:

_____ 4.This character teaches Mandy that wisdom brings

blessings. Bible verse:

Bible verses to choose from:
Proverbs 16:22
*Luke 6:31
Proverbs 16:18
Proverbs 3:13
*Memory verse

Knowledge Is the Best Treasure
Discussion Questions

1. What trick did Marcus play on Mandy? Why do you think Marcus played a trick on her?

2. What happened to Mandy when she took a bite of what she thought was ketchup? What could have happened?

3. What did Mandy's father tell her after she ate the spicy food?

4. What kind of fountain was Mandy's father talking about?

5. Why did Marcus go into the cave? What did he find?

6. Marcus thinks he is the smartest, but how did his actions make him look unwise?

7. What is the Golden Rule?

8. How can you treat others the way you want to be treated?

9. Why are we to treat others with kindness?

10. When someone is hurt, how can you help them?

Name:_____   Date:_____

Knowledge Is the Best Treasure
Word Search

```
Q  J  U  D  G  E  M  E  N  T  Q  G  F  K  U
C  A  U  T  I  O  U  S  S  D  G  H  D  J  N
W  H  G  K  F  O  O  L  I  S  H  H  S  H  D
E  D  E  L  I  C  I  O  U  S  W  J  M  G  E
D  J  F  L  J  R  T  G  F  F  E  K  A  E  R
R  E  D  M  H  C  O  N  F  U  S  E  S  F  S
D  K  C  N  G  E  Y  H  D  G  I  L  L  D  T
A  L  S  I  F  W  U  J  S  H  C  M  N  E  A
N  P  W  I  S  D  O  M  X  J  K  N  D  C  N
G  O  X  B  D  I  I  K  C  K  N  B  Q  E  D
E  I  A  P  O  L  O  G  I  Z  E  V  W  I  I
R  U  L  E  S  S  O  N  V  L  S  C  E  V  N
O  Y  C  V  S  Q  O  L  S  M  S  X  R  E  G
U  K  E  T  C  H  U  P  B  N  E  Z  T  D  P
S  T  I  N  S  T  R  U  C  T  I  O  N  A  Q
```

Foolish	Sickness	Delicious
Apologize	Lesson	Deceived
Caution	Wisdom	Ketchup
Decisions	Confuse	Dangerous
Judgment	Understanding	Instruction

99

Scaredy Crab
Matching Quiz

A.    B.    C.    D.

Match the character to his/her description. Choose one Bible verse from the box that best applies to each statement.

_____ 1. This character tells the girls to pray to Jesus during their sleepover. Bible verse:

_____ 2. This character makes fun of Carter, who is afraid of the storm. Bible verse:

_____ 3. This character says he is afraid of heights. Bible verse:

_____ 4. This character tells her class that the Lord is the stronghold of her life. Bible verse:

| Bible verses to choose from: |
| Matthew 7:12 |
| John 14:27 |
| *Psalm 27:1 |
| Philippians 4:6 |
| *Memory verse |

Scaredy Crab
Discussion Questions

1. What were the students afraid of as they sat in the classroom?

2. Why do you think Carter didn't want to tell anyone he was afraid?

3. What was Carter afraid of doing on the playground? Why do you

   think he was afraid?

4. How do you think Carter felt when he overcame his fear?

5. What are you afraid of sometimes?

6. What is an example of good fear?

7. What is an example of imagined fear?

8. What can you do to be brave?

9. What do you think adults are afraid of?

10. What does Jesus give us when we pray to Him because we are

    worried or anxious?

Name:_____   Date:_____

Scaredy Crab
Word Search

```
F  R  I  G  H  T  E  N  I  N  G  U  I  M  Q
Q  P  A  V  E  K  J  V  B  F  G  Y  O  N  T
L  O  S  C  I  L  A  N  X  I  O  U  S  B  R
I  I  D  X  G  P  P  C  N  D  H  T  P  V  E
G  U  F  Z  H  O  O  X  M  S  J  P  L  C  M
H  H  G  A  T  I  L  Z  P  A  K  R  K  O  B
T  O  H  S  S  T  O  R  M  Q  L  A  J  V  L
N  N  J  J  V  U  G  A  O  W  M  Y  H  E  I
I  E  K  E  B  Y  I  S  I  P  N  E  G  R  N
N  S  L  S  N  T  Z  D  U  E  B  R  F  C  G
G  T  M  U  M  R  E  F  Y  A  V  R  D  O  W
W  Y  N  S  B  R  A  V  E  C  C  E  S  M  E
E  Y  B  X  Q  E  H  G  T  E  X  W  A  E  R
C  L  I  M  B  I  N  G  R  E  Z  Q  Z  X  T
R  T  V  C  W  S  T  R  O  N  G  H  O  L  D
```

Peace	Jesus	Brave
Apologize	Storm	Trembling
Overcome	Lightning	Honesty
Heights	Prayer	Anxious
Climbing	Frightening	Stronghold

A Shocking Fib
Matching Quiz

A.    B.    C.    D.

Match the character to his/her description. Choose one Bible verse from the box that best applies to each statement.

_____ 1. This character lies about another character.

Bible verse:

_____ 2. This character wants to play with the others but is

afraid they don't like him. Bible verse:

_____ 3. This character warns Christian not to believe silly

myths. Bible verse:

_____ 4. This character believes everything that Marcus tells

him. Bible verse:

Bible verses to choose from:
Proverbs 14:15
1 Timothy 4:7
Hebrews 13:6
*Proverbs 19:9
*Memory verse

Name:_____   Date:_____

A Shocking Fib
Discussion Questions

1. What lie did Marcus tell Freddy?

2. Why did Marcus tell a lie about Slim?

3. Why do you think Freddy told the boys what Marcus said about Slim?

4. Why was Slim sad?

5. How was Christian being brave when he spoke with Slim?

6. What did the boys do to scare Marcus?

7. How can telling a lie about someone be dangerous?

8. What does it mean to be tenderhearted?

9. What should you do if someone tells you a lie?

10. Do you know the difference between a lie and the truth?

A Shocking Fib
Word Search

```
S H A R K T O P U S D A S D Q
Q O P N M J H L H F J E S U S
D I R M L K G F O R G I V E T
A U L I K L E K G G S P D H E
N F K S D P L M F H C O H J N
G I J T J I E N D J A I I K D
E B H A H O C B S K R U D L E
R B G K G I T U A P E Y I M R
O I F E F U R V L L D T N N H
U N D B D Y I C Q O S R G B E
S G S V S T C X W O U E F V A
W T A C A R F Z R I D S J C R
G L O W I N G A E U F W G X T
E R Z X Q E D S L I M Q H Z E
M Y T H S W S U R P R I S E D
```

Slim	Jesus	Tenderhearted
Fibbing	Electric	Surprised
Mistake	Scared	Hiding
Ridiculous	Dangerous	Glowing
Forgive	Sharktopus	Myths

110

111

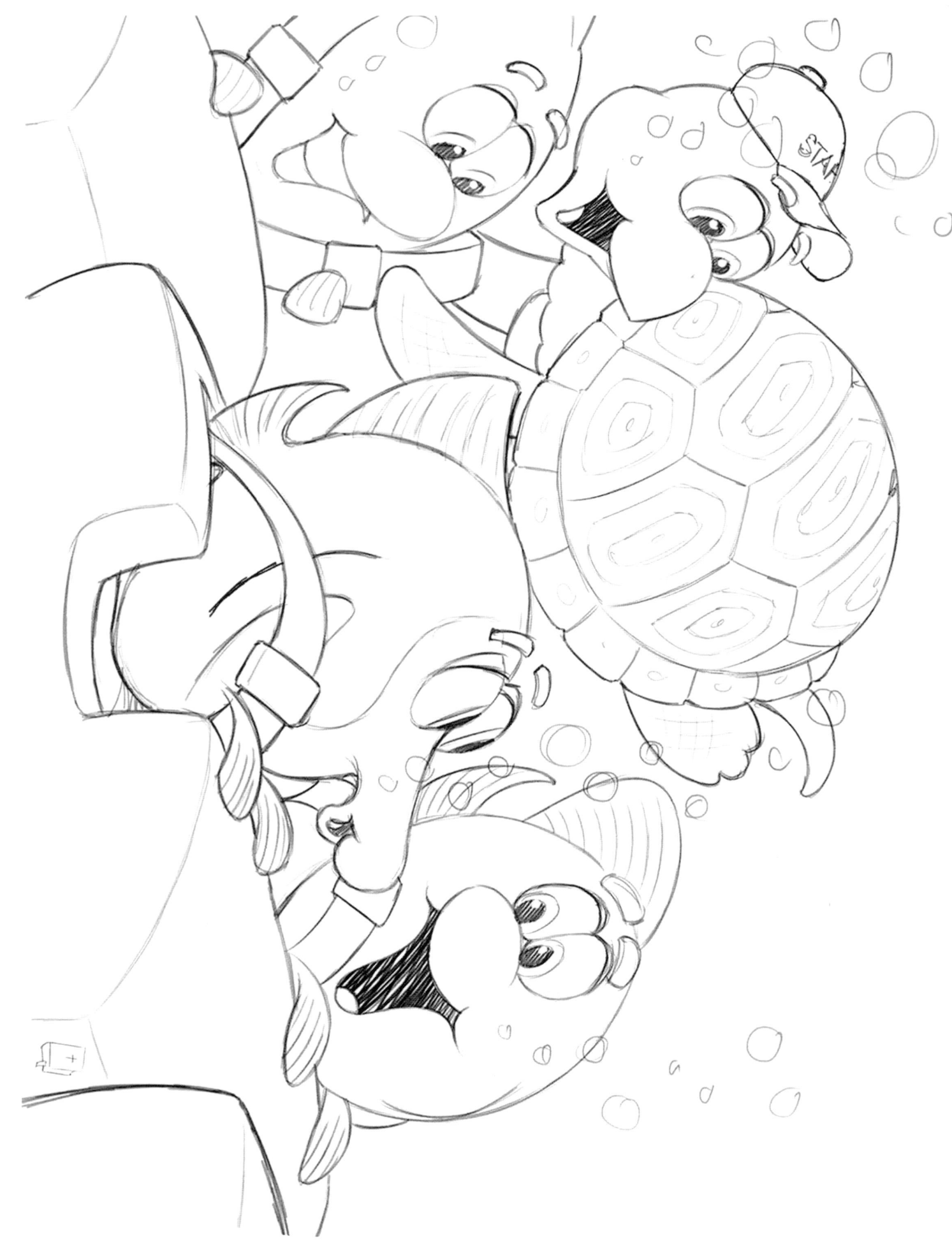

Name: _____   Date: _____

Make your own story with Freddy!

Name:_____   Date:_____

Make your own story with Carter!

Name: _____   Date: _____

Make your own story with David!

Make your own story with Mandy!

Name: _____   Date: _____

Make your own story with Susie!

Name:_____   Date:_____

Make your own story with Melissa!

Answer Sheet

A Servant Like Jesus
Quiz: 1.A; 2.D; 3.B; 4.C

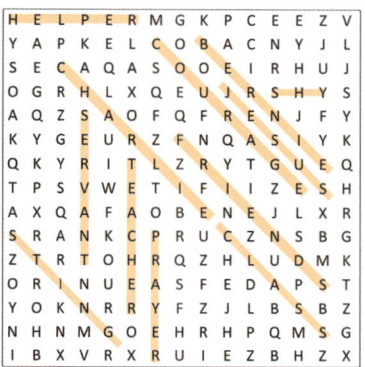

Fast Freddy
Quiz: 1.B; 2.D; 3.B; 4.D

I'm Not Afraid!
Quiz: 1.C; 2.A; 3.C; 4.B

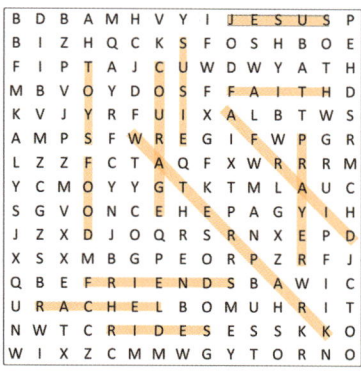

Forever With Jesus
Quiz: 1.C; 2.A; 3.B; 4.C

What a Bragger!
Quiz: 1.A; 2.A; 3.D; 4.C

God's Gift
Quiz: 1.C; 2.D; 3.C; 4.C

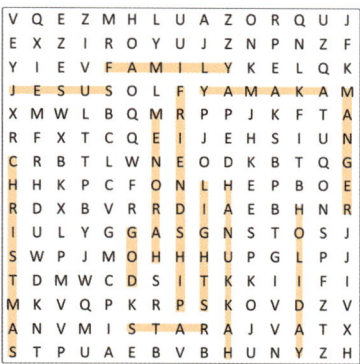

God's Easter Miracles
Quiz: 1.D; 2.B; 3.C; 4.D

Answer Sheet

The Respect Effect

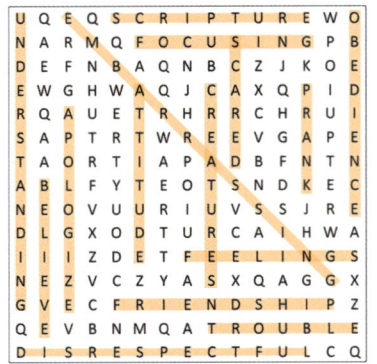

Quiz:
1. B; Ephesians 6:1-3
2. C; 1 Corinthians 15:33
3. D; Romans 13:2
4. A; Proverbs 1:5

Sharing Is Caring

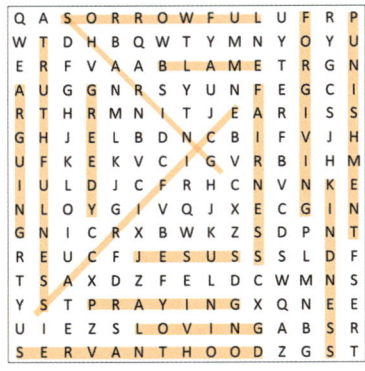

Quiz:
1. C; Hebrews 12:11
2. B; Hebrews 13:16
3. D; 2 Timothy 2:23
4. A; Galatians 5:13

Unique Gifts

Quiz:
1. D; Proverbs 19:29
2. B; Proverbs 18:24
3. A; Hebrews 12:14
4. C; 1 Corinthians 12:17-18

Better Together

Quiz:
1. D; Matthew 5:39
2. B; Proverbs 14:30
3. A; Matthew 5:9
4. C; Luke 6:27

Cleanliness Is Next to Godliness

Quiz:
1. D; Psalm 147:3
2. C; 1 Corinthians 14:40
3. B; Ephesians 5:4
4. A; Galatians 6:2

This Is My Father's World

Quiz:
1. D; Psalm 37:30
2. C; Romans 8:7
3. A; Psalm 24:1
4. B; Luke 21:15

Answer Sheet

Too Much Screen Time

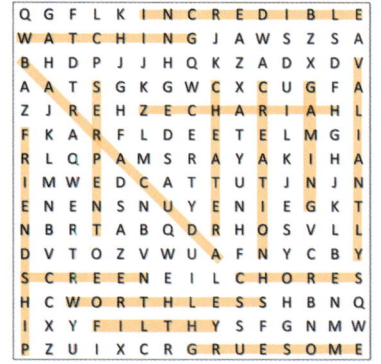

Quiz:
1. A; Zechariah 8:5
2. D; 1 Peter 1:14-15
3. C; Psalm 56:3
4. B; Psalm 119:37

A Thankful Heart

Quiz:
1. D; Hebrews 13:5
2. C; 1 Timothy 4:4
3. B; 1 Thessalonians 5:18
4. A; John 6:12

Love Is the Best Policy

Quiz:
1. C; John 8:32
2. D; Ephesians 4:15
3. B; Proverbs 19:11
4. A; 1 John 3:18

Bible Challenge

Quiz:
1. B; 2 Timothy 3:16
2. A; Matthew 6:33
3. C; Philippians 3:14
4. D; Exodus 30:12

The New Babysitter

Quiz:
1. D; 2 Thessalonians 3:10
2. A; Proverbs 11:17
3. C; James 4:17
4. B; Leviticus 19:18

Church Is for Everyone!

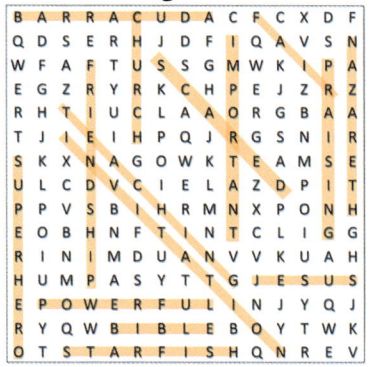

Quiz:
1. D; Hebrews 10:25
2. C; Psalm 150:6
3. B; 1 John 14:26
4. A; Peter 1:15

Answer Sheet

Praying for Puppy

Quiz:
1. A; Psalm 37:30
2. C; Proverbs 13:16
3. B; Proverbs 8:33
4. D; Colossians 3:23

Practice Makes Pretty Perfect

Quiz:
1. D; 1 Thessalonians 2:11
2. A; Proverbs 14:23
3. B; 1 Corinthians 9:24
4. C; James 1:4

Friends First

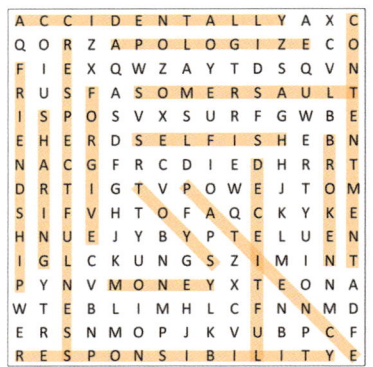

Quiz:
1. B; Hebrews 13:16
2. C; 1 John 3:18
3. D; Psalm 34:13
4. A; Philippians 4:11-13

Safety First

Quiz:
1. C; Romans 12:10-11
2. D; Proverbs 11:14
3. B; Philippians 2:4
4. A; Proverbs 27:12

Grudge or Grace

Quiz:
1. B; John 14:15
2. D; Leviticus 19:18
3. C; Ephesians 4:31
4. A; Psalm 119:11

Faith Over Fear

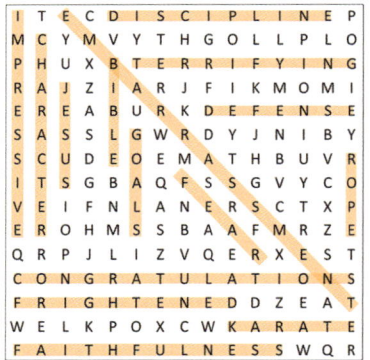

Quiz:
1. A; 1 Samuel 17:45
2. C; 2 Timothy 1:7
3. B; Romans 5:4
4. D; Joshua 1:9

Answer Sheet

The Color of Attention

Quiz:
1. B; Proverbs 3:1
2. A; Proverbs 2:11
3. C; Galatians 6:9
4. D; Proverbs 4:25

Once Lost, Now Found

Quiz:
1. D; Leviticus 19:11
2. A; 3 John 1:4
3. C; 3 John 1:11
4. B; Jeremiah 29:12

The Worrier

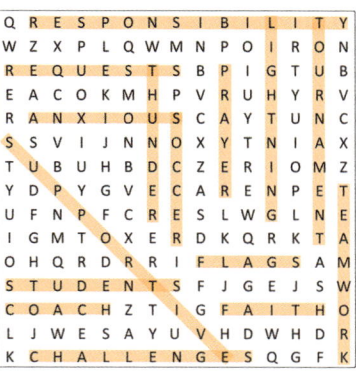

Quiz:
1. B; 1 Peter 5:7
2. D; Matthew 7:7
3. C; Proverbs 15:1
4. A; Philippians 4:16

Stop and Smell the Patience

Quiz:
1. D; Ephesians 4:2
2. C; Philippians 2:14
3. B; 1 Thessalonians 2:7
4. A; Proverbs 2:11

Let Others Shine

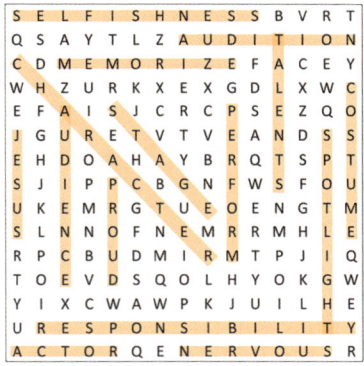

Quiz:
1. A; James 4:6
2. D; Luke 7:28
3. B; Matthew 25:21
4. C; Matthew 18:20

Knowledge Is the Best Treasure

Quiz:
1. D; Proverbs 16:18
2. C; Proverbs 16:22
3. B; Luke 6:31
4. A; Proverbs 3:13

Answer Sheet

Scaredy Crab

F	R	I	G	H	T	E	N	I	N	G	U	I	M	Q
Q	P	A	V	E	K	J	V	B	F	G	Y	O	N	T
L	O	S	C	I	L	A	N	X	I	O	U	S	B	R
I	I	D	X	G	P	C	N	D	H	T	P	V	E	E
G	U	F	Z	H	O	O	X	M	S	J	P	L	C	M
H	H	G	A	T	I	L	Z	P	A	K	R	K	O	B
T	O	H	S	S	T	O	R	M	Q	L	A	J	V	L
N	N	J	J	V	U	G	A	O	W	M	Y	H	E	I
I	E	K	E	B	Y	I	S	I	P	N	E	G	R	N
N	S	L	S	N	T	Z	D	U	E	B	R	F	C	G
G	T	M	U	M	R	E	F	Y	A	V	R	D	O	W
W	Y	N	S	B	R	A	V	E	C	C	E	S	M	E
E	Y	B	X	Q	E	H	G	T	E	X	W	A	E	R
C	L	I	M	B	I	N	G	R	E	Z	Q	Z	X	T
R	T	V	C	W	S	T	R	O	N	G	H	O	L	D

Quiz:
1. C; Philippians 4:6
2. A; Matthew 7:12
3. B; John 14:27
4. D; Psalm 27:1

A Shocking Fib

S	H	A	R	K	T	O	P	U	S	D	A	S	D	Q
Q	O	P	N	M	J	H	L	H	F	J	E	S	U	S
D	I	R	M	L	K	G	F	O	R	G	I	V	E	T
A	U	L	K	L	E	K	G	G	S	P	D	H	E	
N	F	K	S	D	P	L	M	F	H	C	O	H	J	N
G	I	J	T	J	I	E	N	D	J	A	I	K	D	
E	B	H	A	H	O	C	B	S	K	R	U	D	L	E
R	B	G	K	G	I	T	U	A	P	E	Y	I	M	R
O	I	F	E	F	U	R	V	L	E	D	T	N	N	H
U	N	D	B	D	Y	I	C	Q	O	S	R	G	B	E
S	G	S	V	S	T	C	X	W	O	U	E	F	V	A
W	T	A	C	A	R	F	Z	R	I	D	S	J	C	R
G	L	O	W	I	N	G	A	E	U	F	W	G	X	T
E	R	Z	X	Q	E	D	S	L	I	M	Q	H	Z	E
M	Y	T	H	S	W	S	U	R	P	R	I	S	E	D

Quiz:
1. C; Proverbs 19:9
2. A; Hebrews 13:6
3. D; 1 Timothy 4:7
4. B; Proverbs 14:15

Meet the Sea Kids

 Susie

 Susie's mother

 Susie's father

 Susie's grandmother

 January

 June

 Twins' mother

 Twins' father

 Christian

 Christian & Mary's father

Mary

 Carter

Carter's father

Carter's mother

David

David's mother

 Mandy

 Mandy's mother

 Mandy's father

 Melissa

Melissa's mother

 Freddy

 Freddy's mother

 Miss Sally Seahorse

 Marcus

Slim

Coach Crab

 Miss Linda Mermaid

Fritz

 Sarah

 Principal Hammerhead